Animal Stories

Chelsea Kong

© 2024-2025 Chelsea Kong

All rights reserved. All images used in this book are licensed copies from their respectful owners including Jasmine Kong, Freepik, Ghetty Images, Canva, others. This book or any portion thereof may not be reproduced or used in any manner whatsoever without the express written permission of the publisher except for the use of brief quotations in a book review.

Printed in 2024-2025, Made in Toronto, Canada
ISBN: 978-1-998335-07-7
Library and Archives Canada

© 2021 Chelsea Kong, Jasmine Kong

All rights reserved. All images used in this book are licensed copies from their respectful owners including Vectorpocket, Freepik. This book or any portion thereof may not be reproduced or used in any manner whatsoever without the express written permission of the publisher except for the use of brief quotations in a book review.

Printed in 2021, Made in Toronto, Canada
ISBN: 978-1-990399-15-2
Library and Archives Canada

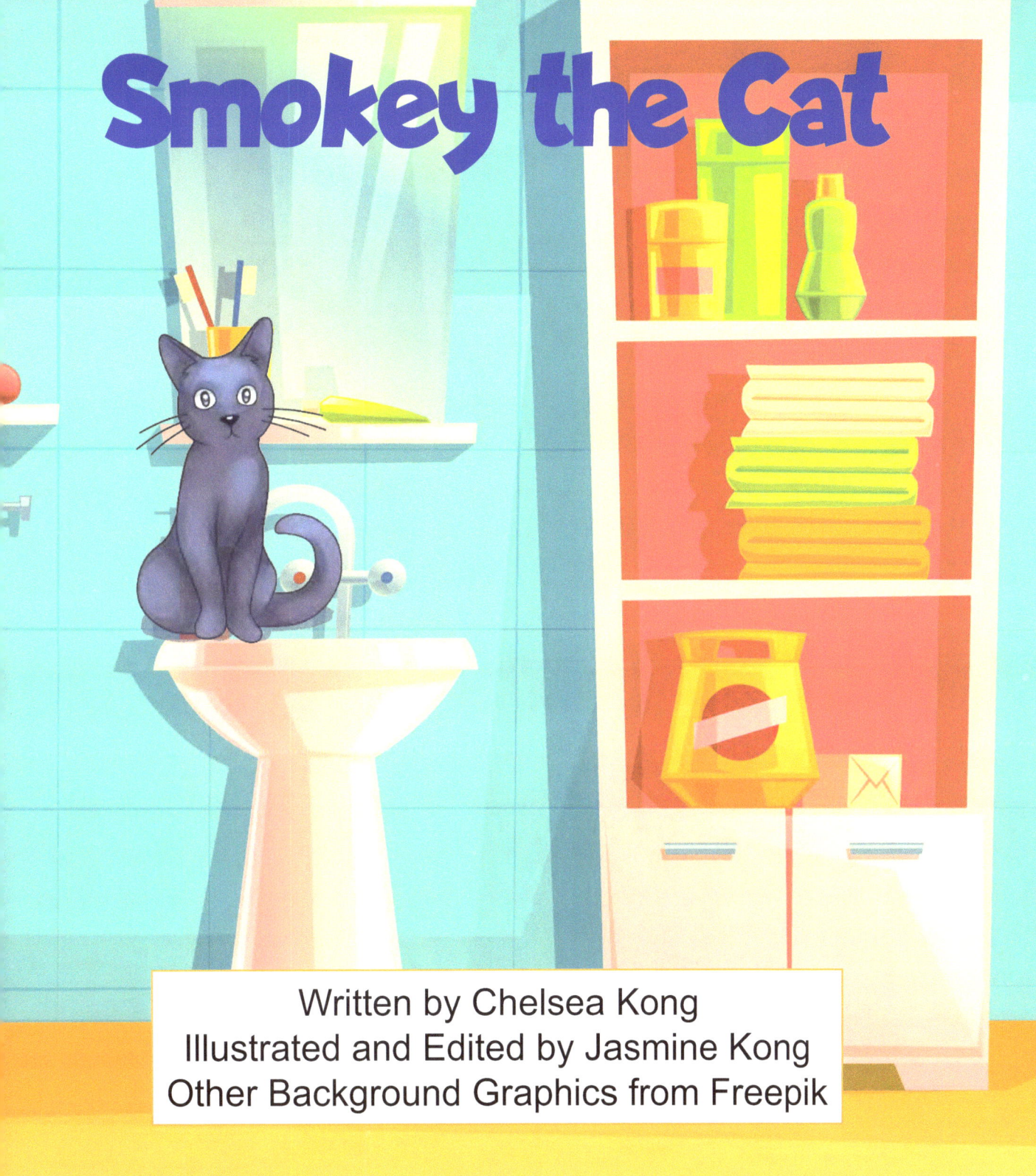

Smokey the Cat

Written by Chelsea Kong
Illustrated and Edited by Jasmine Kong
Other Background Graphics from Freepik

Each day he enjoys his meal and drink
It doesn't take much for him to think

That life is so sweet.

He loves to sleep on the purple bed cover.
The texture like no other.

His favourite toys are large and small.
Oh, he loves them. He loves them all.

The cat dancer, red mouse, and the bumpy green ball.

This cat is a happy loved cat.

He loved to sit on top of the window sill to see outside

Such a surprise to see.
The squirrels, birds, and the trees.

He loves fruits:
Strawberries, blueberries, and cherries!
Yummy and sweet to the taste!

Smokey loves to play hide and seek.
And he hides in the dark.
Where did you go?

Out from the shower, he runs with power!

Up he jumps onto the sink waiting for a drink.

Drippity drip!
Smokey takes a big lick
to taste the water in the sink.

What do you think of that?
A hiss and a growl he makes.

A cookie that is sweet.
What a delightful treat to eat!

He climbs on tables and chairs!
He climbs up and down everywhere!

In a box and under the table!

At the end of day, Smokey rushes with great speed. Purring joyfully.

His favourite cat treat.

He sits on your lap and on your chair.
On your desk and on the stairs.

When he has a need,
he comes with great speed!

Where does Smokey like to sleep?

Content and happy as he can be
There's nothing better than this, you see?

Facts

Russian blue kittens usually have yellow with green rim eyes.
Adults have bright green eyes.
Lifespan: 15-20 years
Male: 10-12 lbs
Female: 7-10 lbs

Cats love cat dancers so that they can be play with you.

They are very smart and need to have toys around to play with.

They are sweet and loyal so you will see them come to greet you when you come home.

Cats can't drink milk or eat what we eat.

They will get sick if they do.

Russian blues have a favourite owner.

They can like everyone and love attention.

Can you connect the dots?

Can you connect the dots?

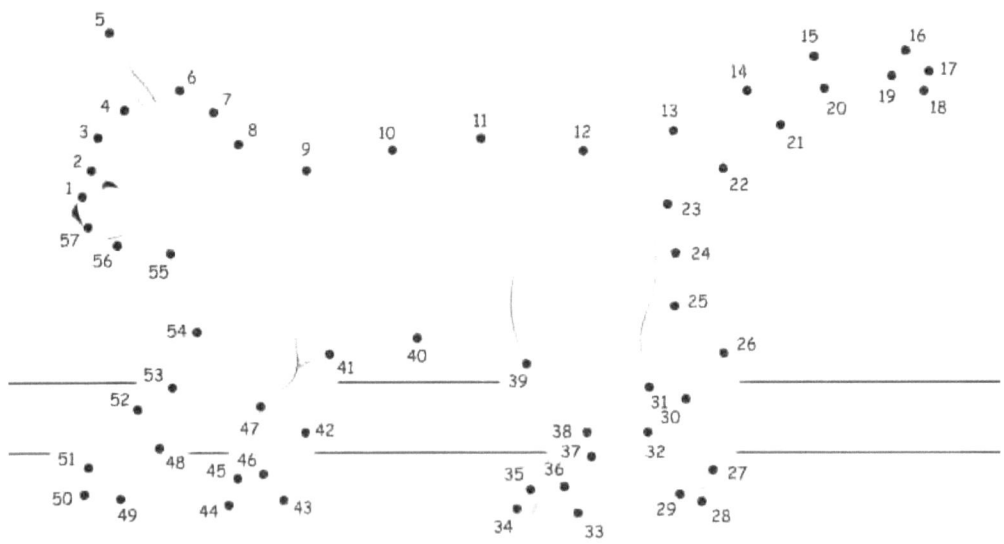

Crossword Puzzle

Horizontal (Across)	Vertical (Down)
[1] The name of the cat (6 letters) [3] Smokey liked to watch the _____ (9 letters)	[2] Smokey likes his red _____ (5 letters) [4] Smokey saw the _____ and the trees (5 letters)

Word Search

Ball Bed Bird	Mouse Smokey Squirrel	Treat Tree

```
W  J  K  P  F  L  I  V  O  N  G  A  M  D
I  Z  H  B  J  M  C  P  K  R  F  Z  O  A
L  N  T  S  M  O  K  E  Y  B  C  H  U  W
L  K  E  X  A  I  G  W  X  D  M  V  S  B
A  Y  Q  V  U  F  B  Z  J  T  R  E  E  C
B  I  R  D  O  E  W  V  Q  H  K  Y  G  L
J  Q  C  G  K  D  X  A  O  P  Z  L  V  F
E  V  A  U  L  E  R  R  I  U  Q  S  C  P
R  C  L  W  H  B  V  O  H  E  J  K  U  H
I  K  T  D  C  S  A  G  P  F  P  D  Q  X
V  F  Q  C  Y  K  D  B  T  A  E  R  T  I
```

Word Match

Smokey is a   mouse
He plays with a   window
He looks outside the   cat
Smokey loves his   purple cover
Smokey sleeps under the   treats

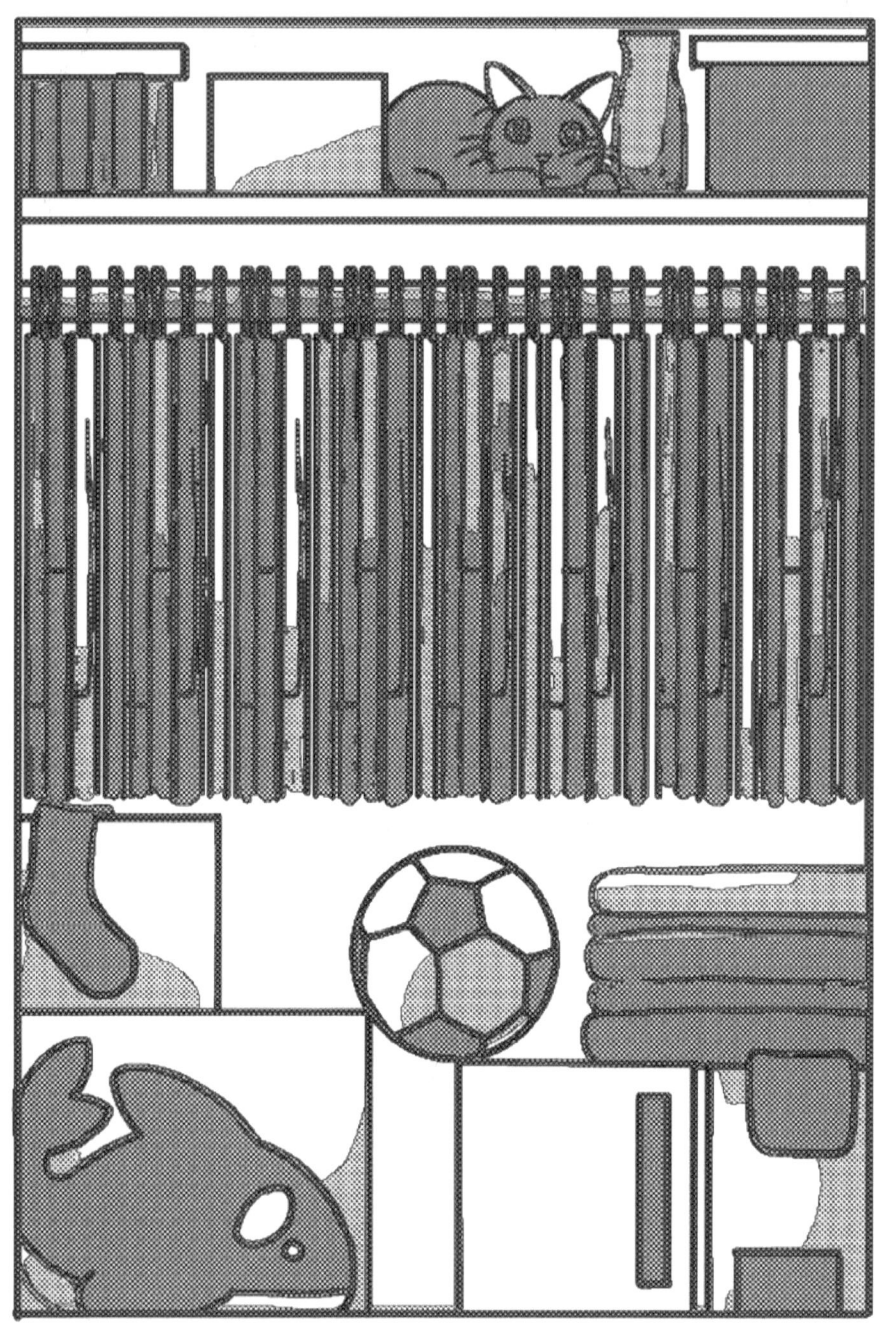

Next, can you find Smokey?

Can you help Smokey get to the rug?

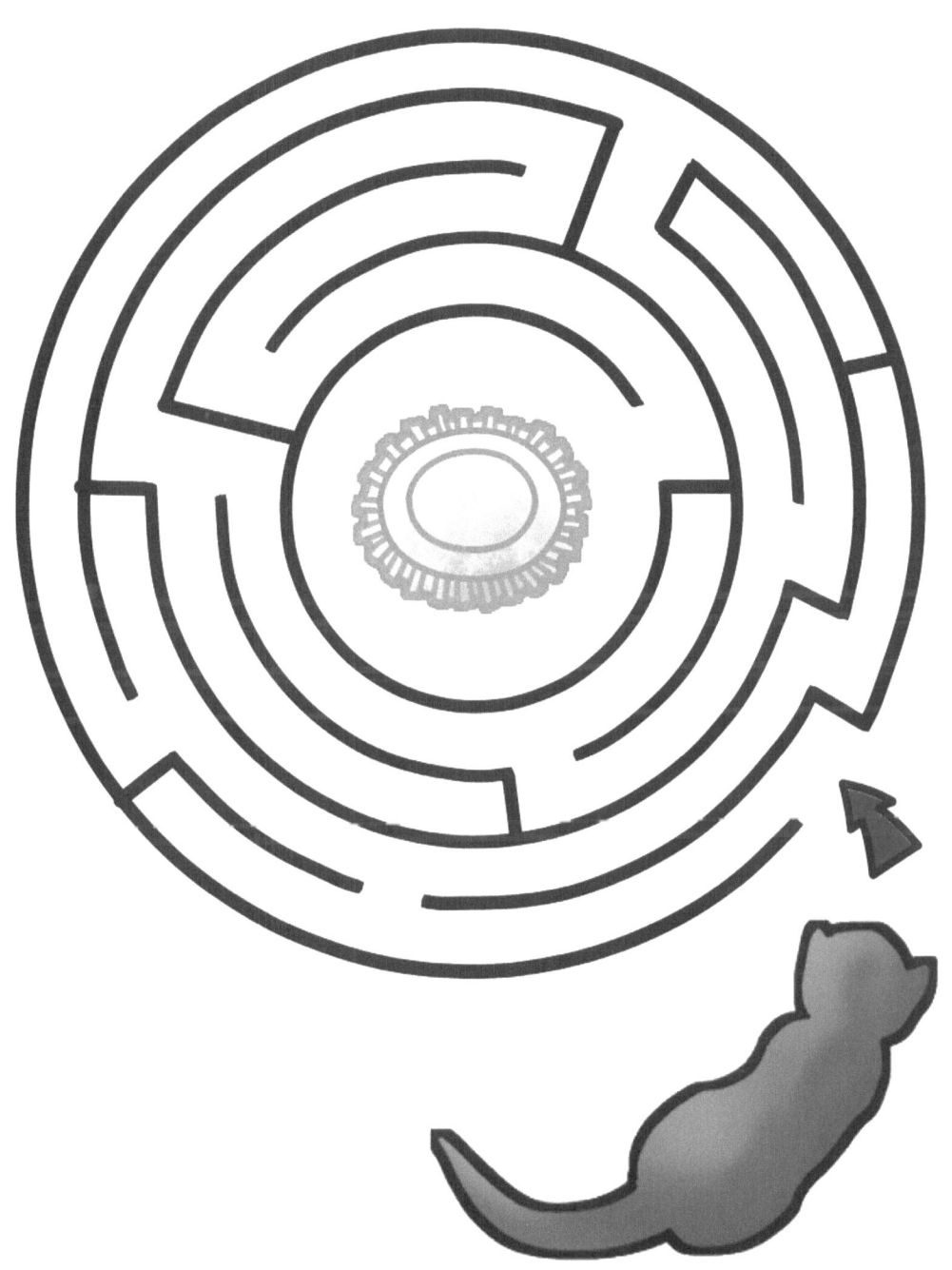

Can you help Smokey out?

Answers

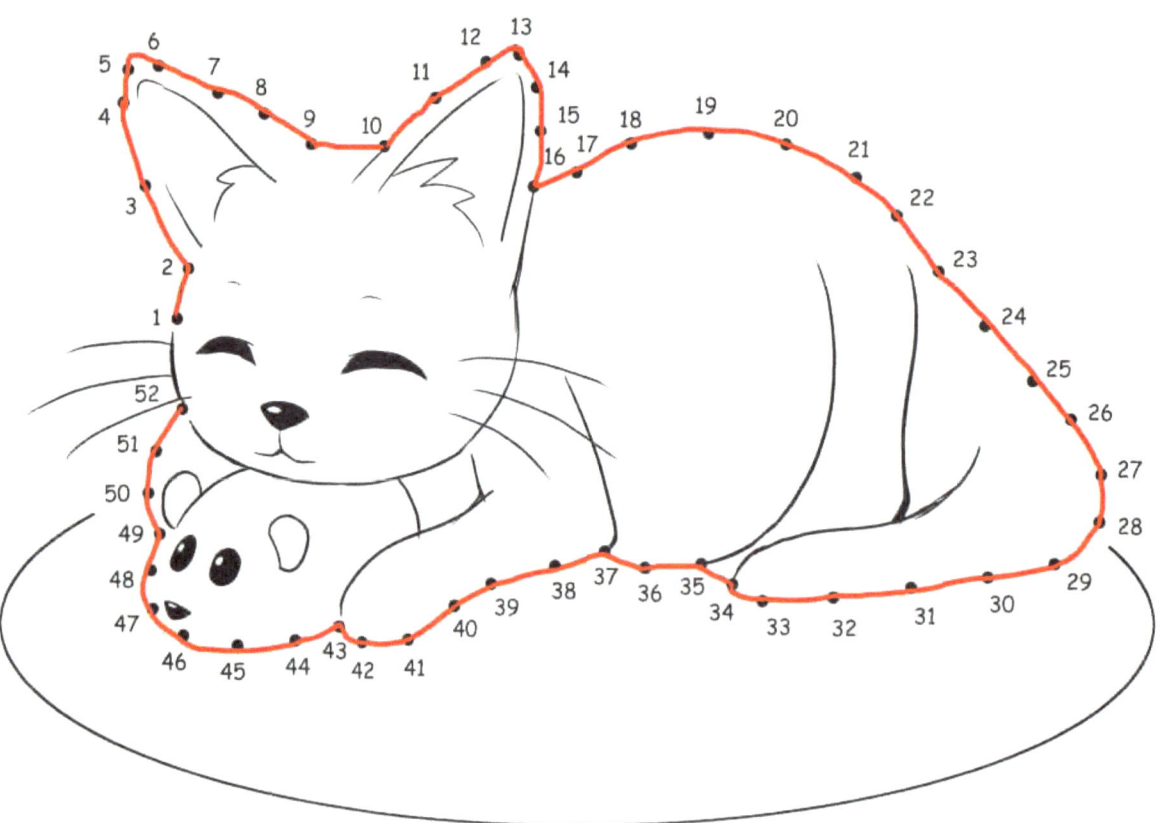

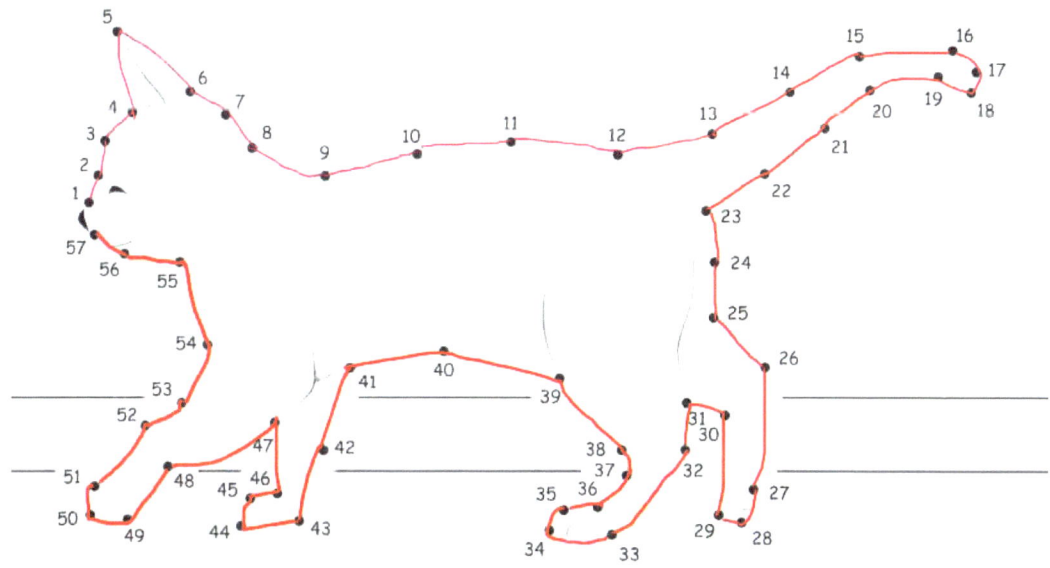

Crossword Puzzle Answers

	¹S	²M	O	K	E	Y				
		O								
		U			⁴B					
		³S	Q	U	I	R	R	E	L	S
		E			R					
					D					
					S					

Horizontal (Across)	Vertical (Down)
¹ The name of the cat (6 letters) ³ Smokey liked to watch the _____ (9 letters)	² Smokey likes his red _____ (5 letters) ⁴ Smokey saw the ____ and the trees (5 letters)

Word Search Answers

Ball Bed Bird	Mouse Smokey Squirrel	Treat Tree

W	J	K	P	F	L	I	V	O	N	G	A	M	D
I	Z	H	B	J	M	C	P	K	R	F	Z	O	A
L	N	T	S	M	O	K	E	Y	B	C	H	U	W
L	K	E	X	A	I	G	W	X	D	M	V	S	B
A	Y	Q	V	U	F	B	Z	J	T	R	E	E	C
B	I	R	D	O	E	W	V	Q	H	K	Y	G	L
J	Q	C	G	K	D	X	A	O	P	Z	L	V	F
E	V	A	U	L	E	R	R	I	U	Q	S	C	P
R	C	L	W	H	B	V	O	H	E	J	K	U	H
I	K	T	D	C	S	A	G	P	F	P	D	Q	X
V	F	Q	C	Y	K	D	B	T	A	E	R	T	I

Word Match Answers

Smokey is a — cat
He plays with a — mouse
He looks outside the — window
Smokey loves his — treats
Smokey sleeps under the — purple cover

Maze Result

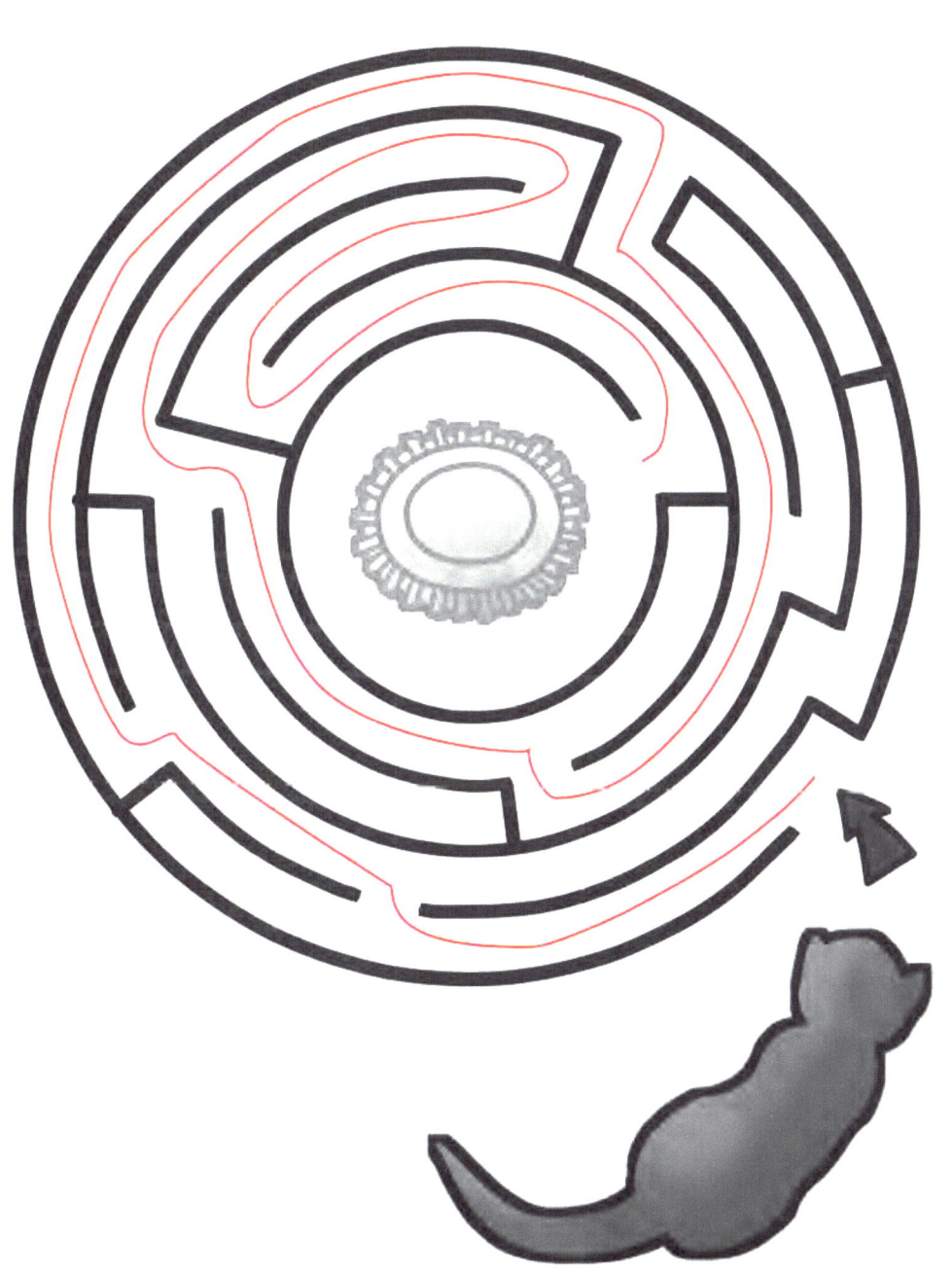

Maze Result

Just to say thanks, you can get a free book here:
https://chelseak532002550.wordpress.com/books-for-sharing/

References

Vanesa Farmer, DVM on July 25, 2022, "What to Know About a Russian Blue Cat." 2005-2024 WebMD.
https://www.webmd.com/pets/cats/what-to-know-about-russian-blue-cat

Cats.com, "Russian Blue Cat."
https://cats.com/cat-breeds/russian-blue

Pandas

CHELSEA KONG

© 2023-2024 Chelsea Kong

All rights reserved. All images used in this book are licensed copies from their respectful owners including Freepik, Ghetty Images, Canva, others. This book or any portion thereof may not be reproduced or used in any manner whatsoever without the express written permission of the publisher except for the use of brief quotations in a book review.

Printed in 2023-2024, Made in Toronto, Canada
ISBN: 978-1-998335-05-3
Library and Archives Canada

Pandas cute and kind.
They put a smile on your mind.

But can you find two of a kind?
Even if there are two alike

They don't act the same.

They love to eat and play.
Then sleep the rest of the day!

Rain or shine.
Fall or snow.

Babies are so cute!
Adults are so big!

They like show.
How fun they can be!

What else can I say?
There is more to know.

Climbing and sliding.
Hiding and lying down.

Water for the adults.
2-3 gallons a day!

Milk for the cubs.
A tasty drink!

Bamboo, so crunchy and tasty too!

Apples and carrots a yummy treat!
Don't forget the bread and the meat!

Pandas love it all!

What about red pandas?
What do they like?

Cute and furry.
They run in a hurry.

They climb and play in the tree.
High and tall!

Fruits a treat that can't be beat!
Bamboo that they always eat.

Be aware that you share.
Red pandas don't care.

Make them mad.
That is bad!

A scary face.
That's not a good place to be.

Be kind.
Then they won't mind.

Now let's have some fun!
Let's see what you know.

Giant Panda Facts

Animal Type: Mammal
Type of Diet: Omnivore
Average life in the wild: 20 years
Average life in the zoo: 30 years
Height: 4 to 6 feet
Weight: 300 pounds

Food: Bamboo shoots and leaves, eggs, apples, carrots, ground meat, special vitamin bread, ginseng, flowers, and fungus.

Bamboo forests are home to pandas.
Southwest China is home to mountains covered in rain.
In a day, they spend 12 hours eating.
Bamboo is the main food, but they may eat fish and small mammals too.
Digestion only processes about a fifth of it.

Pandas stay healthy by eating at least 15% of their body weight.
Their teeth can eat bamboo shoots, leaves, and stems.
Pandas are great climbers, reaching heights of up to 13,000 feet, and they are also good swimmers.

Male pandas find females by aroma.
Females follow breeding time.
A female panda needs 2-3 months to carry a baby panda inside.
There aren't many pandas left in the world.

A baby panda needs 90-184 days to be born. In the first 2-3 weeks, mother panda uses her front paws and thumb-like wrist to hold the baby. Pandas can bear twins and triplets.

Baby pandas are blind at birth and have a thin white coat and look pink. Their eyes open about 45 days. They can walk at 75-80 days old.

They stay inside from 100 to 120 days.
At 14 months, they can eat bamboo.
At 18-24 months, they can be alone.

Red Panda Facts

Animal Type: Mammal
Type of Diet: Omnivore
Average life: 8-10 years
Height: 22 to 25 inches
Weight: 8-17 pounds
Food: Bamboo shoots and leaves and fruits

Red Panda Facts

They climb on trees and can grab fast.
They are like weasels, raccoons, and skunks.
They live mainly in the trees and mountains
of Nepal, Myanmar and Central China.

Red Panda Facts

Their special thumb-like wrist bone
helps them to grab when they climb.
They know how to keep balance on tree limbs.

Red Panda Facts

They can hide in the trees.
Their feet helps them rotate
180 degrees backwards.

Red Panda Facts

Both red pandas and cats lick themselves. There is little fur on the bottom of the baby red, panda's feet.

Red Panda Facts

They use their tail to keep warm when it's cold.
Every day, they eat about 20,000 bamboo leaves.
Red pandas also like fruit.

Red Panda Facts

A red panda cub weighs about 3.5 ounces.
They are shy unless they mate.
There are only 10,000 in the world.

Let's see how how much you know.

Panda Word Search

Apples
Bamboo
Eat
Milk

Panda
Play
Sleep
Water

Giant Panda Word Search

B	L	E	H	O	P	L	A	N	C	
K	R	J	C	G	T	I	N	R	O	
D	P	A	N	D	A	G	K	E	D	
C	U	L	N	B	E	J	Y	T	S	
P	N	F	A	D	C	V	J	A	E	
E	N	D	T	Y	I	G	N	W	L	
E	B	A	M	B	O	O	F	Z	P	
L	O	F	I	Q	J	Y	G	H	P	
S	C	H	L	N	Z	E	T	U	A	
U	B	X	K	A	C	U	H	E	V	

Red Panda Word Search

China
Cleans
Climbs
Cute

Fruit
Nepal
Red Panda
Trees

Red Panda Word Search

R	L	A	P	E	N	L	A	K	S
E	K	S	Z	C	H	I	N	A	N
D	E	A	O	T	Q	G	W	J	A
P	T	L	N	B	R	J	C	B	E
A	U	F	Q	D	S	E	V	P	L
N	C	D	R	F	B	G	E	Q	C
D	O	Y	H	U	M	N	B	S	U
A	L	F	T	J	I	Y	G	H	T
U	M	H	Z	A	L	T	Q	L	F
V	B	X	F	O	C	D	H	Z	J

Giant Panda Crossword

Across

2. These bears eat bamboo and leaves.

5. Pandas love to do this.

6. Pandas _____ the trees.

Down

1. Panda's favourite food.

3. The place where the giant panda lives.

4. Favourite treat to eat.

7. They like to drink this.

Red Panda Crossword

Red Panda Crossword

Across

2. They know how to _____ on trees.

5. They eat bamboo _____ and shoots.

Down

1. Red Pandas can be found in a place that begins with M.

3. They are like weasels, skunks, and this animal.

4. They live in in a place that begins with N.

6 They _____ their fur like cats.

7. They like to climb on _____.

Giant Panda's Scrambled

Unscramble to get the answer.

Adpan

Abobom

Hsif

Rtrscoa

Vesela

Serte

Klmi

Etraw

Red Panda's Scrambled

Unscramble to get the answer.

Der Ndapa

Uftir

Iachn

Bmicl

Yrmanam

Cnaleba

Nepal

Aypl

Answers

Giant Panda Word Search

B	L	E	H	O	P	L	A	N	C
K	R	J	C	G	T	I	N	R	O
D	P	A	N	D	A	G	K	E	D
C	U	L	N	B	E	J	Y	T	S
P	N	F	A	D	C	V	J	A	E
E	N	D	T	Y	I	G	N	W	L
E	B	A	M	B	O	O	F	Z	P
L	O	F	I	Q	J	Y	G	H	P
S	C	H	L	N	Z	E	T	U	A
U	B	X	K	A	C	U	H	E	V

Red Panda Word Search

R	L	A	P	E	N	L	A	K	S
E	K	S	Z	C	H	I	N	A	N
D	E	A	O	T	Q	G	W	J	A
P	T	L	N	B	R	J	C	B	E
A	U	F	Q	D	S	E	V	P	L
N	C	D	R	F	B	G	E	Q	C
D	O	Y	H	U	M	N	B	S	U
A	L	F	T	J	I	Y	G	H	T
U	M	H	Z	A	L	T	Q	L	F
V	B	X	F	O	C	D	H	Z	J

Giant Panda Crossword

Giant Panda's Scrambled

Unscramble to get the answer.

Panda

Bamboo

Fish

Carrots

Leaves

Trees

Milk

Water

Giant Panda's Scrambled
Unscramble to get the answer.

Red Panda

China

Myanmar

Nepal

Fruit

Climb

Balance

Play

References

National Geographic Kids, "Giant Panda"
National Geographic, 2015-2024
https://journeynorth.org/tm/eagle/facts_ecology.html

Britannica, "Giant Panda" Britannica, 2024
https://www.britannica.com/animal/giant-panda

National Geographic Kids, "Red Panda"
National Geographic, 2015-2024
https://kids.nationalgeographic.com/animals/mammals/facts/red-panda

CELIA'S BIRTHDAY

CHELSEA KONG

© 2024-2025 Chelsea Kong

All rights reserved. All images used in this book are licensed copies from their respectful owners including Jasmine Kong, Freepik, Ghetty Images, Canva, others. This book or any portion thereof may not be reproduced or used in any manner whatsoever without the express written permission of the publisher except for the use of brief quotations in a book review.

Printed in 2024-2025, Made in Toronto, Canada
ISBN: 978-1-998335-06-0
Library and Archives Canada

It is finally Celia's birthday!
She got so excited.

Birthdays are a special time of the year.

What do you do on yours?

Most people celebrate it only once a year.

Make your birthday special with some cheer!

Did you know it opens the way for blessings to flow?

Be thankful and joyful every day!

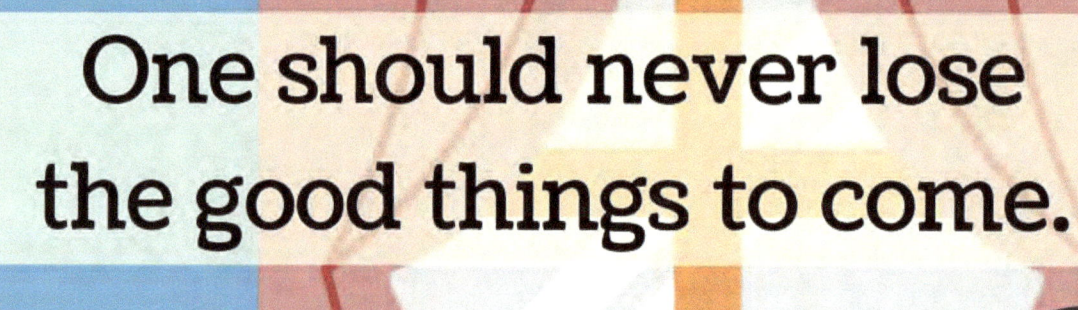

One should never lose the good things to come.

Helping others and share.
Always bless others.

There is so much more
for you and me to explore!

Then you will receive that which your heart desires.

Birthdays open the door for so much more!

Happy Birthday

Friends who share will always care for you.

Blessings have power.
That will shower over you.

Keep on giving and not just taking all you can get.

More will come.
That is so much more fun.

More to explore than you know!

Even in the ocean floor.
There is beauty all around.

Hare Facts

LIFE: 4-8 YEARS AND SOMETIMES UP TO 12 YEARS.
SIZE: GROWS UP TO 40-70 CENTIMETRES (2.4 TO 4.3 INCHES).
FOOD: GRASS, FRUITS, VEGETABLES, SEEDS, NUTS, AND SOME FUNGI.

Hare Facts

THEIR SPEED: 70 KILOMETRES
OR 43 MILES PER HOUR.
WITH LONGER EARS AND TALLER HIND
LEGS, THEY LOOK LARGER RABBITS.
HARES LIVE ABOVE GROUND.

Hare Facts

A BABY RABBIT IS CALLED A BUNNY.
THE MALE RABBIT IS JACK.
THE FEMALE RABBIT IS JILL.

Hare Facts

HARES ARE FOUND IN EURASIA, AFRICA, NORTH AMERICA AND JAPANESE ARCHIPELAGO.

Hare Facts

THEIR HIND LEGS ARE POWERFUL
AND CAN LEAP MORE
THAN 3 METRES OR 10 FEET.
THEY SLEEP IN THE DAYTIME.

Hare Facts

THE SNOWSHOE HARE HAS FUR THAT TURNS WHITE TO HELP THEM HIDE.
IN SPRING, THEIR FUR IS SHORTER AND LOOKS MORE BROWN.
HARES LIKE TO LIVE ALONE AND LIKE TO STAY AWAKE AT NIGHT.

Hare Facts

THEY STAY CLOSE TO THE GROUND AND MAKE THEIR EARS LIE FLAT ON THEIR BACKS

Hare Facts

FEMALE HARES ARE READY TO HAVE BABIES FOR 42 DAYS.
THEY HAVE TO 1-8 BABIES AT A TIME.
EACH YEAR, THEY CAN HAVE THREE LITTERS.

Hare Facts

JACK RABBITS ARE HARES.
THEY ARE BROWN.
YOUNG HARES CALLED LEVERETS CAN
HOP A FEW MINUTES AFTER BIRTH.

Rabbit Facts

EAR LENGTH: GROWS UP TO 10 CENTIMETERS AND TURNS 180 DEGREES THEY HAVE LONG EARS, BIG HIND LEGS, AND SHORT FUR.
FOOD: GRASS, WILDFLOWERS AND VEGETABLES (CARROTS AREN'T THAT GOOD FOR THEM.)

Rabbit Facts

A BABY RABBIT IS CALLED A KIT.
THE MALE IS CALLED A BUCK.
THE FEMALE IS CALLED A DOE.

Rabbit Facts

THEY CAN JUMP HIGH.
THEY HAVE SHARP HEARING.
THEIR TEETH KEEP GROWING.

Rabbit Facts

THEY LIKE TO LIVE IN GROUPS. THEY LIVE IN WARRENS (MADE OF MANY TUNNELS AND ROOMS DUG UNDERGROUND).

Rabbit Facts

MOTHER RABBITS ARE READY TO HAVE A BABY FROM 28 TO 31 DAYS. THEY HAVE UP TO 14 BABY RABBITS AT ONE TIME: CALLED KITTENS

LET'S SEE WHAT YOU REMEMBER BY DOING SOME ACTIVITIES!

Activities

Hare Word Search

Alone
Above
America
Hare

Leap
Longer
Night
Taller

Hare Word Search

C	L	F	Z	R	E	L	L	A	T
Z	K	P	H	T	D	Y	Q	U	D
Q	J	A	B	O	V	E	W	J	C
P	R	E	Q	C	S	J	V	B	X
E	U	L	O	N	G	E	R	P	E
N	C	T	R	F	B	G	E	Q	N
D	O	Y	H	U	M	N	C	S	O
J	L	F	T	G	D	Y	G	H	L
U	M	H	A	C	I	R	E	M	A
V	B	X	F	O	Z	N	H	Z	J

Rabbit Word Search

Buck
Doe
Grass
Hides

Jump
Kit
Rabbit
Tunnels

Rabbit Word Search

R	L	X	K	E	N	L	Y	K	D
F	K	C	Z	C	X	I	B	Q	O
P	U	A	O	B	H	Z	W	J	E
B	T	L	N	T	I	K	C	U	V
C	P	F	Q	O	D	G	V	M	L
N	Y	D	J	F	E	U	A	P	C
D	G	R	A	S	S	N	Q	W	U
Z	L	C	Q	J	P	Y	V	L	T
U	M	T	I	B	B	A	R	D	F
S	L	E	N	N	U	T	H	Z	J

Hare Crossword

Across

2. They know how to _____ on trees.

5. They eat bamboo _____ and shoots.

Down

1. Red Pandas can be found in a place that begins with M.

3. They are like weasels, skunks, and this animal.

4. They live in in a place that begins with N.

6 They _____ their fur like cats.

7. They like to climb on _____.

Hare Crossword

Rabbit Crossword

Across

1. Hare is _____ than rabbits.

4. They like to live _____.

7. They love to ____ high.

Down

2. The like to live _____ ground.

3. There ears are _____ than rabbits.

4. You can find them in a place the starts with A.

6 The opposite of day.

8. A baby Jack and Jill belongs to a ____.

Rabbit Crossword

Hare Scrambled
Unscramble to get the answer.

Earh

Noeal

Grearl

Ongl

Vobea

Ceraiam

Lleart

Htign

Rabbit Scrambled
Unscramble to get the answer.

Briatb

Mpuj

Itk

Kcub

Oed

Teeth

Esnunlt

Usogpsr

LET'S SEE HOW YOU DID!

Answers

Hare Word Search

C	L	F	Z	R	E	L	L	A	T	
Z	K	P	H	T	D	Y	Q	U	D	
Q	J	P	B	O	V	E	W	J	C	
P	R	E	Q	C	S	J	V	B	X	
E	U	L	O	N	G	E	R	P	E	
N	C	T	R	F	B	G	E	Q	N	
D	O	Y	H	U	M	N	C	S	O	
J	L	F	T	G	D	Y	G	H	L	
U	M	H	A	C	I	R	E	M	A	
V	B	X	F	O	Z	N	H	Z	J	

Rabbit Word Search

R	L	X	K	E	N	L	Y	K	D
F	K	C	Z	C	X	I	B	Q	O
P	U	A	O	B	H	Z	W	J	E
B	T	L	N	T	I	K	C	U	V
C	P	F	Q	O	D	G	V	M	L
N	Y	D	J	F	E	U	A	P	C
D	G	R	A	S	S	N	Q	W	U
Z	L	C	Q	J	P	Y	V	L	T
U	M	T	I	B	B	A	R	D	F
S	L	E	N	N	U	T	H	Z	J

Hare Crossword

Rabbit Crossword

Hare Scrambled
Unscramble to get the answer.

Hare

Alone

Larger

Long

Above

America

Taller

Night

Rabbit Scrambled
Unscramble to get the answer.

Rabbit   **Doe**

Jump   **Teeth**

Kit   **Tunnels**

Buck   **Groups**

References

National Geographic Kids, "10 Hopping Fun Rabbit Facts." National Geographic Kids, 2015-2024
https://journeynorth.org/tm/eagle/facts_ecology.html

Tons of Facts, "27 Fun and Interesting Facts About Hares." 2020 Tons of Facts
http://tonsoffacts.com/27-fun-interesting-facts-hares/

Britannica, "Hare." Animals & Nature
https://www.britannica.com/animal/hare-mammal

MESSAGE FROM THE AUTHOR

Thank you for reading this book. I hope you can leave a good review to encourage me to write more books to teach children and adults. I wanted children to enjoy the stories about animals that I wrote in one book. I am glad that you took the time to read this one! Please share my books with your friends to enjoy too!

OTHER PRODUCTS

- Knowing God
- How to Hear God's Voice
- New Life in Jesus
- Loving Israel
- God's Gifts/Spiritual Talents
- Meeting God
- Word Power
- Fruit of the Spirit
- The Tabernacle
- Bride for Jesus
- A Life of Prayer
- Live Free
- Who am I in Jesus
- Walk in Love
- God's Favor
- Man of God
- Woman of God
- How to Use Money
- God's Wisdom
- Fasting
- See Jerusalem and Bethany
- First Fruit Offering
- Feast of Trumpets
- Day of Atonement
- Feast of Tabernacles
- Counting the Omer
- Festival of Lights
- Glory, Presence, and Holy Spirit
- Live in God's Presence
- Pentecost
- See Galilee, Nazareth, and Tiberias
- Hear God Speak
- Knowing Jesus
- Knowing Holy Spirit
- A Healthy Life and Healthy Life Work Book
- Smokey the Cat
- Passover Unleavened Bread
- Resurrection Life
- The Blessing
- Revival
- Chelsea Learns Hebrew
- Thanksgiving
- Give Thanks
- Jesus Birth
- Loving Jesus: Bride and Groom
- Proverbs 31 Woman

OTHER PRODUCTS

ABC of People in the Bible
Colours in the Bible
Breakthroughs
Open Doors
The Seven Spirits of God
Numbers in the Bible
Aglee the Eagle
An Eagle's Life
Chelsea Learns Numbers in Hebrew
ABC's of Faith
Feast of Purim
A Royal Life
Chelsea Learns Numbers in Hebrew
ABC's of Faith
Feast of Purim
A Royal Life
Pandas
Worship
Celia's Birthday

Devotionals
31 Day Devotional

Inspirational/Other
Chelsea's Psalms and Poems
Your Daily Meal: Chelsea's Photo Album
Chelsea's Psalms and Poems2
Travel West Caribbean

Puzzle Books
Biblical Puzzle Book Vol 1-5
Bible Puzzles for Young Children Book 1-3
Biblical Puzzle for Children Books 1-5

OTHER PRODUCTS

Teaching Series
How to Hear God's Voice Teaching Guide & Audio Book
Relationship with God, Jesus, Holy Spirit Guide
Knowing God, Jesus, Holy Spirit Guide & Audio Book
Flowing in the Prophetic

Teaching (Non-Sale on my website)
Purim
Passover
Resurrection

BOOK REVIEWS

More books on Amazon, Kobo, and Barnes and Noble, Smashwords, and IngramSpark.
https://chelseak532002550.wordpress.com/

More books on Amazon, Kobo, and Barnes and Noble, Smashwords, and IngramSpark.
https://www.amazon.com/author/chelseakong

Please leave a review and share with friends to help the author continue to write more books to reach more readers. Thank you so much for your support.

About
CHELSEA KONG

She is a writer, creative arts and digital media artist, skilled administration and payroll professional, and podcaster. Chelsea also served in a variety of roles, from audiovisual, photography, to assisting on the worship team, and ministry team. She also has a passion for families being united.

Chelsea has been a guest on Unity Live Radio, The Lady Tracey Show, and How to Live for Christ and is highly recommended by a Proud Christian blog. She is also a guest blogger. A few of her books have been featured in YourAuthorHub, etc. She graduated from Hotel and Restaurant Management, Digital Media Arts, Office Administration, Payroll Professional, and experience working with children. Chelsea lives in Toronto, Canada. She mainly writes children's books, stories, bridal writing, poems, lyrics for songs, words of encouragement, blessings, prayers, and jokes. The author of How to Hear the Voice of God, the Bridal Collection, Knowing God, etc. She also has her own Bible Puzzle books and other inspired products. Her podcast channel is called Chelsea K on Anchor, Spotify, and iTunes.

Please check my website to find out more:
https://chelseak532002550.wordpress.com/

About
JASMINE KONG

She is a self-employed artist in graphics, web, and gaming. She graduated from Tradigital Animation and has studied Graphic Design. She produces her own graphics for commissions. Her graphics range from simple to more complicated. Her favourite art style is anime and she enjoys watching Japanese anime. She also produces graphics suitable for websites. She has also been featured in an anime book and won first prize for the contest. Everyone who knows about her artwork enjoys it. She has even had an opportunity to show students how to do a bit of origami.

www.ingramcontent.com/pod-product-compliance
Lightning Source LLC
Chambersburg PA
CBHW060811010526
44116CB00003B/44